William Richard Morfill

A Simplified Grammar of the Polish Language

William Richard Morfill

A Simplified Grammar of the Polish Language

ISBN/EAN: 9783743393547

Manufactured in Europe, USA, Canada, Australia, Japa

Cover: Foto ©Paul-Georg Meister /pixelio.de

Manufactured and distributed by brebook publishing software
(www.brebook.com)

William Richard Morfill

A Simplified Grammar of the Polish Language

TRÜBNER'S COLLECTION

OF

SIMPLIFIED GRAMMARS

OF THE PRINCIPAL

ASIATIC AND EUROPEAN LANGUAGES.

EDITED BY

REINHOLD ROST, LL.D., Ph.D.

———

XI.

POLISH.

BY W. R. MORFILL, M.A.

TRÜBNER'S COLLECTION OF SIMPLIFIED GRAMMARS OF THE PRINCIPAL ASIATIC AND EUROPEAN LANGUAGES.

EDITED BY REINHOLD ROST, LL.D., Ph.D.

Grammars of the following are in preparation :—
Albanese, Anglo-Saxon, Assyrian, Bohemian, Bulgarian, Burmese, Chinese, Cymric and Gaelic, Dutch, Egyptian, Finnish, Hebrew, Khassi, Kurdish, Malay, Pali, Russian, Sanskrit, Serbian, Siamese, Singhalese, &c., &c., &c.

LONDON: TRÜBNER & CO., LUDGATE HILL.

A

SIMPLIFIED GRAMMAR

OF THE

POLISH LANGUAGE.

BY

W. R. MORFILL, M.A.

LONDON:

TRÜBNER & CO., LUDGATE HILL.

1884.

GILBERT AND RIVINGTON, LIMITED,
ST. JOHN'S SQUARE, CLERKENWELL ROAD.

CONTENTS.

CHAPTER III.

PREFACE.

The following short Grammar is the first attempt of the kind in English. It is to be hoped that it may be instrumental in furthering the study of Polish, a noble language, which is still spoken by about ten millions of people. I have consulted with advantage previous works on the subject, written in Polish, German and French. I have found the " Comparative Grammar " of Miklosich, the " Historico-Comparative Grammar " of Malecki (2 vols., Lemberg, 1879), and the works of Orda (Paris, 1856) and Rykaczewski (Berlin, 1861) very useful. Following the plan of the " Simplified Grammars," I have only given an outline of the language, but this outline will be found to contain all the chief rules, which I have endeavoured to make as plain as possible. The student of comparative philology will thus be able to form a correct idea of the structure of the language, and it may serve as a rudimentary handbook to any one who is anxious to read the works of such authors as Mickiewicz and Krasinski in the original.

W. R. MORFILL.

Oxford.

Example 3 :—*koń*, 'the horse.'

Singular.	*Plural.*
N. koń	konie.
G. konia	koni (ów).
D. koniowi	koniom.
A. konia	konie.
V. koniu	konie.
I. koniem	koniami (końmi).
L. koniu	w koniach.

Among peculiar forms belonging to this declension may be mentioned the noun *Bóg*, 'God,' which makes the dative *Bogu*, instead of *Bogowi*, and also the vocative *Boże;* *człowiek*, 'man,' has in the vocative both *człowieku* and *człowiecze;* *xiądz*, 'priest,' has the genitive *xięże*.

SECOND DECLENSION.

Feminine substantives are those ending in the vowels *a* (except a few implying the offices of men) and *i*, and most of the substantives ending in one of the soft consonants *ć, dź, ść, ź, ż*.

Example 1:—*pani*, ' the lady.'

Singular.	*Plural.*
N. pani	panie.
G. pani	pań.
D. pani	paniom.
A. panią	panie.
V. pani	panie.
I. panią	paniami.
L. pani	paniach.

Example 2 :—*praca*, 'labour.'

Singular.	Plural.
N. praca	prace.
G. pracy	prac.
D. pracy	pracom.
A. pracę	prace.
V. praco	prace.
I. pracą	pracami.
L. pracy	pracach.

Example 3 :—*żona*, 'the wife.'

Singular.	Plural.
N. żona	żony.
G. żony	żon.
D. żonie	żonom.
A. żonę	żouy.
V. żono	żony.
I. żoną	żonami.
L. żonie	żonach.

Example 4 :—*część*, 'the part.'

Singular.	Plural.
N. część	części.
G. części	części.
D. części	części om.
A. część	części.
V. części	części.
I. częścią	częściami.
L części	częściach.

THIRD DECLENSION.

Neuter Substantives.

To this declension belong all the neuter substantives ending in *e, ę, o.* These neuter nouns differ from masculines, with the same termination; in the neuters the nominative, accusative and vocative are the same in both numbers: in the plural these cases end in *a.*

Example 1 :—*pole,* ' the field.'

Singular.	*Plural.*
N. pole	pola.
G. pola	pól.
D. polu	polom.
A. pole	pola.
V. pole	pola.
I. polem	polami.
L. polu	polach.

Example 2 :—*cielę,* ' the calf.'

Singular.	*Plural.*
N. cielę	cielęta.
G. cielęcia	cieląt.
D. cielęciu	cielętom.
A. cielę	cielęta.
V. cielę	cielęta.
I. cielęcięm	cielętami.
L. cielęciu	cielętach.

Example 3 :—*imie,* ' the name.'

Singular.	*Plural.*
N. imie	imiona.
G. imienia	imion.
D. imieniu	imionom.
A. imie	imiona.
V. imie	imiona.
I. imieniem	imionami.
L. imieniu	imionach.

To this declension belong the verbal substantives in *ie,* but, as a rule, they are only used in the singular.

Many other substantives are also used only in the singular, especially when a collective idea is implied; as, *żyto,* 'barley;' *jazda,* 'cavalry;' *dziatwa,* 'children.' Others are only used in the plural; as, *chrzciny,* 'baptism;' *łowy,* 'hunting.' Substantives can also be modified into diminutives and augmentatives; as, *krówka,* 'a little cow;' *mieścisko,* 'a great ugly town.' In some substantives in the last syllable in the locative *a* and *o* are changed into *e,* as *gniazdo,* ' the nest,' *w gniezdie; siodło,* 'the saddle,' *w siedle; jezioro,* 'the lake,' *w jezierze; żelazo,* 'the iron,' *w żelazie.*

The following substantives are also irregular :—*oko,* 'the eye;' *ucho,* 'the ear,' in the plural; *xiąze,* 'prince,' is irregular in the singular—in the plural it is declined like *cielęta,* 'calves.'

tańszy, 'cheapest.' The superlative of pre-eminence is made by placing *bardzo*, 'very,' before the adjective, as *bardzo dobry*, ' very good.'

NUMERALS.

Cardinal.

1. Jeden.		11. Jedenaście.	
2. Dwa.		12. Dwanaście.	
3. Trzy.		13. Trzynaście.	
4. Cztéry.		14. Czternaście.	
5. Pięć.		15. Piętnaście.	
6. Sześć.		16. Szesnaście.	
7. Siedm.		17. Siedemnaście.	
8. Ośm.		18. Ośmnaście.	
9. Dziewięć.		19. Dziewiętnaście.	
10. Dziesięć.		20. Dwadzieścia.	

Dzieście, or *dzieści*, is added to the numerals from twenty to fifty, *piędziesiąt;* from fifty to one hundred, *dziesiąt* being added. Thus, *cztérdzieści*, ' forty,' *dziewięć-dziesiąt*, 'ninety.' The smaller numerals follow the greater as in English; as *trzydzieści pięć*, 'thirty-five ;' *ośmdziesiąt siedm* ' eighty-seven.'

100. Sto.	600. Sześćset.
200. Dwieście.	700. Siedemset.
300. Trzysta.	800. Ośmset.
400. Czterysta.	900. Dziewięćset.
500. Pięćset.	1000. Tysiąc.

The arrangement of the greater and smaller numerals is the same as in English : thus, *sto dwadzieścia siedm*, ' one hundred and twenty-seven.' *Jeden, jedna, jedno* are declined after the manner of adjectives.

Dwaj, ' two.' *

N. dwaj (*a*), dwa (*b*).	N. dwie (*c*).
G. dwóch.	G. dwóch.
D. dwóm.	D. dwóm.
A. dwóch (*a*), dwa (*b*).	A. dwie.
I. dwoma.	I. dwiema.
L. dwoch.	L. dwóch.

Trzej, ' three.'

Czterej, ' four.'

N. trzey (*a*), trzy (*d*).	N. czterej (*a*), cztery (*b*).
G. trzech.	G. czterech.
D. trzem.	D. czterem.
A. trzech (*a*), trzy (*d*).	A. czeterech (*a*), cztery (*d*)
I. trzema.	I. czterema.
L. trzech.	L. czterech.

---

* Following the example of Rykaczewski, and in order to secure brevity in the above tables, letters have been used for, (*a*) men, (*b*) animals of the masculine gender, and inanimate objects masc. and neuter ; (*c*) women, and all feminine substantives ; (*d*) substantives of whatsoever gender they may be, except signifying men. According to their position with these, the numerals are modified.

Pięciu, ' five.'

N. pięciu (a), pięc (d).   A. pięciu (a), pieć (d).

G. pięciu.   I. pięcią.

D. pięciu.   L. pięciu.

Jeden, dwaj, dwa, dwie, trzej, trzy, czterej, cztery are considered as adjectives, and in consequence the substantive goes with them in the nominative case. *Dwaj, trzej,* and *czterej,* however, are only so used when they precede their nouns; if they follow them the noun is put in the genitive, as *miast dwa,* ' two cities.' *Pięć* and the rest up to *tysiąc* are substantives, and take a genitive case after them.

Jedenastu, ' eleven.'

N. jedenastu (a), jedenaście (b).   A. jedenastu (a), jedenaście (d).

G. jedenastu.   I. jedenastą.

D. jedenastu.   L. w jedenastu.

Pięciudziesiąt, ' fifty,' inflects the word *pięciu* (as given previously) : the word *dziesiąt* remains unaltered. All the numerals till *czterdjieści* are declined like *jedenascie,* and all the others till *dziewięcdziesiąt* like *pięćdziesiąt.*

Stu, ' a hundred.'

Singular.	*Plural.*
N. stu (a), sto (d).	sta.
G. sta *or* stu.	set.
D. stu.	stom.
A. stu (a), sto (d).	sta (d).
I. stem.	stami.
L. stu.	stach.

c

Dwustu, 'two hundred.'

N. dwustu (*a*), dwieście (*d*).	A. dwóchset (*a*), dwieście (*d*).
G. dwóchset.	I. dwomaset, dwiemaset (*c*).
D. dwómset.	L. dwóchset.

For the others, *e.g.* 500, take the word *pięc,* as previously declined, and add in each case *set.*

Tysiąc, 'a thousand.'

Singular.	*Plural.*
N. tysiąc.	tysiące.
G. tysiąc a	tysięcy.
D. tysiącu.	tysiącom.
A. tysiąc.	tysiące.
I. tysiącem.	tysiącami.
L. tysiącu.	tysiącach.

The ordinal numbers are not given here, as they are inflected like adjectives, and can be easily learned from a dictionary. In the Slavonic languages we also find collective numerals, as *czworo*, 'a collection of four;' *piecioro dzieci,* 'a band of five children.' *Cf.* English, 'a dozen,' 'a score.' These collective numerals take for the most part the genitive case after them.

THE PRONOUNS.

PERSONAL.

Singular.

Ja, ' I.'		Ty, ' Thou.'
N. ja.		N. ty.
G. mnie.		G. ciebie.
D. mnie, mi.		D. tobie, ci.
A. mnie, mię.		A. ciebie, cię.
V. ja.		V. ty.
I. mną.		I. tobą.
L. mnie.		L. tobie.

Plural.

N. my, 'we.'		N. wy, 'you.'
G. nas.		G. was.
D. nam.		D. wam.
A. nas.		A. was.
V. my.		V. wy.
I. nami.		I. wami.
L. nas.		L. was.

Singular.

N. on, ' he.'	ona, ' she.'	ono, ' it.'
G. jego, go, niego.	jej, niej.	jego, go, niego.
D. jemu, mu, niemu.	jej, niej.	jemu, mu, niemu
A. jego, go, niego.	ją, nią.	je, nie.
I. nim.	nią.	niem.
L. nim.	niej.	niem.

Plural.

For Men.	For all except Men.
N. oni, 'they.'	one, ' they.'
G. ich, nich.	ich, nich.
D. im, nim.	im, nim.
A. ich, nich.	je.
I. nimi.	niemi.
L. nich.	_ nich.

The abridged forms of the pronouns are only used after verbs, and cannot be employed after prepositions, or when emphasis is to be laid upon the pronoun.

The pronoun *niego* is sometimes changed into *ń* in the genitive and accusative, and is united with the preposition, as *dlań* for ' him ;' so also the pronoun *ci* is changed into *c*, and is attached to a previous word ending in a vowel.

The pronoun *siebie, się* is reflexive : it is used to express the singular and the plural of all three genders, and may refer to all three persons.

G. siebie, się.	I. sobą.
D. sobie.	L. sobie·
A. siebie, się.	

The POSSESSIVE PRONOUNS are declined like adjectives, as *mój*, ' my,' *twój*, ' thy ;' for the third person the genitive singular and plural of the personal pronoun is used, as *jego, ich*.

DEMONSTRATIVE PRONOUNS.

Ten, 'this.'

Singular.

N. ten,	ta,	to.
G. tego,	tej,	tego.
D. tem,	tej,	temu.
A. tego, ten,	tę,	to.
I. tym,	tą,	tem.
L. tym,	tej,	tem.

Plural.

Men.	For all others.
N. oni.	one.
G. onych.	onych.
D. onym.	onym.
A. onych.	one.
I. onymi.	onemi.
L. onych.	onych.

RELATIVE PRONOUNS.

Kto, co, który, która, które are both relatives and inter-rogatives. *Kto* refers to masculines and feminines; *co* to animals and inanimate things: they have no plural. *Który* is declined like an adjective, the only irregularity being *którzy* for the masculine nominative plural.

The NEGATIVE PRONOUNS when employed with verbs require also the use of the negative particle. Several letters and words may be added to pronouns, which have the effect of modifying their meanings, as *ś, kolwick, li, lito, ż, że, żeto* : *ś* and *kolwiek* are added only to pronouns, as *ktoś, jakiś, ktokolwiek,* &c. ; *li, lito, ż, że, żeto* are added not only to pronouns but to adjectives.

THE VERBS.

Since a great object has been simplification as much as possible, I shall here only enumerate the chief divisions of the verbs :—

1. *Active.*

2. *Passive.* In reality there is no independent form of the passive voice in Polish. It is made, as in most modern European languages, by the auxiliaries and the past participle. See, however, on p. 49 as to the various ways of expressing this voice.

3. *Neuter.*

4. *Impersonal.*

5. *Perfect,* sometimes called Completive Verbs, which express the action as finished; e.g., *zjadłem,* ' I have ceased eating.'

6. *Imperfect,* or Continuative Verbs, which express the duration of the action ; e.g., *jem,* ' I continue to eat.'

7. *Inceptives,* which express an increasing action; as *starzeję się,* 'I grow old.'

8. *Frequentatives*, which express an action continually repeated, as *jadam*, 'I eat frequently.' Both active and neuter verbs may be either *dokonane* or *niedokonane*, perfect or imperfect. The perfect verbs have no present tense nor any present participle.* The mark of the perfect verb is the future anterior, as it is called, which is conjugated like the present of the imperfect verbs ; e. g., *zgadnę*, 'I shall have guessed ;' *przyczytam*, 'I shall have finished reading.'

Many perfect verbs are characterized by being compounded with a preposition, which gives the idea of completion ; others by changes in the letters. Perfect verbs are sometimes formed out of imperfect by changing the termination *ać* into *ić* or *ąć*. The two forms, perfect and imperfect, make a complete conjugation in Polish. We must ascertain to which of these two classes a verb belongs by looking into a good dictionary. Frequentatives, as a rule, form the present in *wam*, the perfect in *wał*, and the infinitive in *wać*. The four last of these divisions are termed by Slavonic grammarians 'aspects.' The constant use of the aspects amply atones for the poverty of tenses in the modern Slavonic verb, in Polish the palæo-Slavonic aorist being lost.

The following are the chief prepositions which enter into the composition of the Polish verbs :—

Do—which implies carrying the action to the extremity ; as *dobić*, ' to beat utterly.'

---

* Małecki, i. 263.

Na—expresses direction towards a certain place, as *pły-wać* ' to sail,' *napływać*, ' to sail towards.'

Nad—expresses excess, as *dać*, ' to give,' *naddać*, ' to give too much.'

Od—expresses distance from a place, as *jechać*, ' to depart,' *odjechać*, ' to go from a place.'

Po—expresses continuation of an action, as *bielić*, ' to make white,' *pobielić*, ' to continue to make white.'

O, ob, obe—express the accomplishment of an action, as *siodłać*, ' to saddle,' *osiodłać*, ' to finish saddling a horse.'

Pod—expresses ' underneath,' like the Latin *sub*, as *pisać*, ' to write,' *podpisać*, ' to sign.'

Prze—express the thorough accomplishment of the action, Latin *per*, as *czytać*, ' to read,' *przeczytać*, ' to read from beginning to end.'

Przy—expresses ' nearness,' as *biedz*, ' to run,' *przybiedz*, ' to run by the side of.'

Roz—expresses different directions, as *pisać*, ' to write,' *rozpisać*, ' to write in different directions.'

U—expresses thoroughness, as *śmiać się*, ' to laugh,' *uśmiać się*, ' to laugh out and out.'

W—expresses direction of a thing within, as *chodzić*, ' to go,' *wchodzić*, ' to go in.'

Wy—expresses ' out,' as *prosić*, ' to entreat,' *wyprosić*, ' to obtain from a person by entreaty.'

W, wz—expresses ' on high,' as *nosić*, ' to carry,' *wznosić*, ' to carry on high.'

Z, ze—expresses the perfect accomplishment of an action, as *jeść*, ' to eat,' *zjeść*, ' to eat entirely.'

Za—expresses ' over,' as *mowić*, ' to speak,' *zamowić*, ' to talk a person over.'

The tenses are, (1) the Present, as *czynię, idę*, &c. (2) The Perfect; as *czyniłem*, ' I did :' really a past participle with certain suffixes, as will be shown afterwards, and hence it is inflected according to gender. (3) The Pluperfect, rarely used; as *czyniłem był*, ' 1 had done.' (4) The Future, which may be expressed in two ways, either by the auxiliary and the participle, as *będę czynił*, or the auxiliary and the infinitive, *czynić będę*—this is the simple future; when sometimes the present is used as a future (*e.g.* in the perfect verb), it is called the future anterior.

The perfect, imperfect, frequentative verbs, &c., are arranged under the four conjugations according to their terminations.

In Polish there are four conjugations and six moods : (1) the Infinitive ; (2) the Indicative ; (3) the Imperative ; (4) the Subjunctive, which is expressed by adding *żeby, ażeby* and *iżby* to the participial form, as *żebym kochał*, ' that I may love.' In reality no Slavonic language has an independent form of the subjunctive. (5) The Conditional, implying a condition : this mood is expressed in Polish in two ways, (*a*) with *by, gdyby, aby*, with the participial form of the verb *być*, ' to be ;' or (*b*) by the addition of *by* to the participial form of the verb in *ł*, but the particle *by* must then take the personal terminations, as *kochał bym*, ' I should have loved.' (6) The Optative, which is made by the conjunction *obym* with the participial form in *l*, as *obym list odebrał*, 'Oh, that I could receive the letter!' Thus we see that in reality there are only three moods in Polish of independent form: the last three are made by particles.

The reader will observe the following elements of the Polish verb :—

The mark of the 1st per. sing. is *m*, which sometimes by a phonetic law becomes *ę*; parallels to these two forms being found in all the Slavonic languages. Sometimes both forms are found in the same verb, as *wydziubywam* and *wydziubuję*; the latter, however, is the more common. Of the second *ś*, or *sz*; of the first person plural *śmy*, of the second *ście.** These may enter into various combinations, and by paying attention to their positions the acquisition of a knowledge of the verbs may be much simplified. These suffixes are in reality, as might be imagined, merely mutilated parts of the present tense of the verb 'to be,' which oldest form was as follows :—

jeśm	jeśmy
jeś	jeście
jest.	są.

---

* The original suffix for the third person singular was *t*; this, however, though preserved in Russian, is lost in the West-Slavonic languages. The suffix of the third person plural is *n*; this, however, by its coalescing with the *bindevocal*, becomes *ę*.

The explanation of the form now in use will be given a little further on.

But these particles can be used not only with verbs but with other words, so as to cause the sentence to be shaped in many different ways, and this peculiarity of the Polish language is deserving of careful consideration; thus we may say either *dobrze pisałem*, or *dobrzem pisał*, 'I have written well,' *ja pilny jestem*, or *jam pilny jest*, 'I am industrious;' *wczora rano byłeś w kościele*, or *wczora ranoś był w kościele*, 'Thou wert early at church yesterday.' So also *my byliśmy*, or *myśmy byli*, 'We were;' *wy byliście*, or *wyście byli*, 'Ye were;' *głośno śpiewaliście*, or *głosnoście śpiewali*, 'You have sung loudly;' &c. They may also be added to particles, as *Bom nie przyszedł wzywać sprawiédliwych ale grzesznych do pokuty*, 'I came not to call the righteous but sinners to repentance.' (Matt. ix. 13.) So also *Ale abyście wiedzieli, iż ma moc syn człowieczy*, 'But that ye may know that the Son of man hath power.' (Matt. ix. 6.) This gives extraordinary flexibility and variety to the sentence.

The following are the suffixes of the Imperative:—

> *Singular* ... 2 pers., *j*.
>
> *Plural* ... $\begin{cases} 1 \text{ pers., } jmy. \\ 2 \text{ pers., } icie. \end{cases}$

The suffix of the Perfect is *ł*, which is added immediately to the stem, as *grał, piekł*. The only exceptions are *kłól, pról*, where the *o* is the connecting vowel (*bindevocal*). This is properly a participle, as is shown by the feminine and neuter terminations and the plural form.

The suffix of the Infinitive is *ć*, which is generally added immediately, but in some instances with a *bindevocal*; from the fusing of *k* with *ć* we get *c*, and from *g* the combination *dz*. The spelling of the termination of the infinitive in some cases in *dż* is censured by Miklosich as inaccurate (iii. 450).

The suffix of the Active Participle is *ąc*. The suffix is originally *nc*, and the addition of a *bindevocal* makes it *ąc*; e. g. *piekąc, trąc.* When the participle is used adjectively it is declined like an adjective—*piekący, -a -e, trący -a -e.*

The suffix of the Perfect Gerund is *szy*; but this is not added immediately to the stem, but after the *l* of the perfect, as *upiekłszy* (*u-piek-l-szy*); or with the addition of *w*, e. g. *wygrawszy* (*wy-gra-w-szy*): this, however, is only another form of *l*, which is frequently pronounced as *w* in Slavonic dialects.

The suffix of the Passive Participle is either -*n*, or -*ł*, which is declined like an adjective, either -*ny, -na, -ne*, or -*ły, -ta, -te.*

The Verbal Substantive is derived from the Passive Participle by adding *ie* to *n* or *t*; e. g. *bity, bicie.* If the *bindevocal* before *ny* has become *o*, it is changed again into *e* before *nie*; e. g. *pieczony, pieczenie, niesiony, niesienie.*

The Indicative Mood has the following tenses: the present, in perfect verbs the future anterior, the pluperfect, and the future. The Subjunctive, Conditional and Optative have only the perfect tense.

Conjugation of Auxiliary Verbs.

być, ' to be.'

INDICATIVE MOOD.

Present.

Singular.

Jestem		jesteś.	·		jest.

Plural.

Jesteśmy		jesteście.		są.

Perfect.

Singular.

Masc.		Fem.		Neut.
Byłem.		byłam.		byłom.
Byłeś.		byłaś.		byłoś.
Był.		była.		było.

Plural.

Byliśmy.		byłyśmy.		byłyśmy.
Byliście.		byłyście.		byłyście.
Byli.		były.		były.

Pluperfect (but little used).

Singular.

Masc.	Fem.	Neut.
Byłem był.	byłam była.	byłom było.

And so on, adding *był* to the masculine, *była* to the feminine, and *było* to the neuter, in all the different persons.

Plural.

Byliśmy byli, adding *byli* to the other persons.	byłyśmy były, adding *były*.	same as feminine.

Future.

Singular.

Będę, 'I shall be.'	będziesz.	będzie.

Plural.

Będziemy.	będziecie.	będą.

CONDITIONAL.

The Conditional Mood is formed from the participial form in *l* and the particle *by ;* after which are added the letters and combinations *m, s, śmy, ście,* to designate the persons. There is no present tense. Thus the perfect (1st. pers.) would be *byłbym, byłabym, byłobym.*

SUBJUNCTIVE.

This Mood is formed by the participial form in *l* (*był*), before which is used the conjunction *żeby* ; to which the letters and combinations *m, ś, śmy, ście* are added, as *żebym był*, 1st person, *żebyś była* (feminine). There is no present, and the pluperfect is omitted here as being so little used.

OPTATIVE.

This resembles in form the Conjunctive, with the difference that *oby* is used instead of *żeby*, and takes the same terminations to mark the persons. The perfect is the only tense used.

IMPERATIVE.

Singular.

Bądź, ' be thou,'—Bądźcie.

Niech or niechaj bądźcie ' let him be.'

To niech and niechaj, the suffix *że* is sometimes added.

Plural.

Bądźmy.	bądźmyż.
Bądźcie.	bądźcież.

Niech *or* niechaj będą.

PARTICIPLES.

Present.

Masc.	Fem.	Neut.
Będący.	będąca.	będące.

Past.

Był y.	była.	było.

Future.

Mający być.	mająca być.	mające być.

Będąc, 'being ;' bywszy, ' having been.'

These two last are not inflected.

The modern form of the present tense of the verb *być* is merely a corruption, and arose from adding to the third person of the old form the pronominal suffixes. This resulted from false analogy, as the suffixes had become fused with the participial form *był, była, było*, and made a past tense ; thus *był jesm* had become *byłem, byli jesmy, byliśmy*.

The particle *by*, which is used in Polish and other Slavonic languages to express condition, was originally the third person singular of the old perfect of the verb *być*, a tense which is now lost. This particle has at the present time something like the use of the Greek ἄν. We also find it in composition as *aby, żeby, ażeby*, with which we may compare Greek ὅταν and ἄν in other combinations.

Mieć, 'to have.'

INDICATIVE MOOD.

Present.

Sing... Mam.	masz.	ma.
Plur... Mamy.	macie.	mają.

Perfect.

Singular.

Masc.	Fem.	Neut.
Miałem.	miałam.	miałom.
Miałeś.	miałaś.	miałoś.
Miał.	miała.	miało.

Plural.

Masc.	Fem.	Neuter.
Mieliśmy.	miałyśmy.	miałyśmy.

(In the second person add the usual suffix: the third person has no suffix.)

Pluperfect.

The same as the preceding tense, adding *był* to the masc. sing., *była* to the fem., and *było* to the neuter; *byli* for masc. plur., and *były* for fem. and neuter.

D

Future.

Singular.

Masc.	Fem.	Neuter.
Będę miał *or* mieć.	będę miała *or* mieć.	będę miało *or* mieć.
Będziesz.	będziesz.	będziesz.
Będzie.	będzie.	będzie.

Plural.

Będziemy mieli *or* mieć.	będziemy miały.	
Będziecie.	będziecie miały.	*ibid.*
Będą.	będą miały.	

CONDITIONAL.

Perfect Tense.

Masc.	Fem.	Neuter.
Miałbym.	miałabym.	miałobym.

Add the regular suffixes to the first and second persons as above, and add the suffixes to the plural, which will be *mieloby* for the masc., and *miałyby* for the fem. and neut.; thus, *mielobiśmy*, &c.

SUBJUNCTIVE.

Add *żeby*, with suffixes for each of the persons, to the ordinary past tense *miał*, in its various mutations of gender and number.

OPTATIVE.

Add *oby*, with the same suffixes.

IMPERATIVE.

Singular.

Miej, 'have thou,'—Miejże.

Niech *or* niechaj (with addition sometimes of suffix *że*)—ma.

Plural.

Miejmy.

Miejcie.

Niech *or* niechaj mają.

PARTICIPLES.

Present.

Masc.		Fem.		Neuter.
Mający.		mająca.		mające.

Perfect.

Miany.		miana.		miane.

Future.

Mający mieć.		mająca mieć.		mające mieć.

Note.—The verb *mam* (I have) is frequently used with merely a future signification, as *wydanie ma być ozdobione trzema portretami*, 'The edition will be furnished with three portraits.'

GERUNDS.

Mając, 'having.'

Miawszy, 'having had.'

Conjugation of Regular Verbs.

FIRST CONJUGATION.

The mark of the conjugation is the second person singular present of the verbs *niedokonane,* or the future anterior of the verbs *dokonane,* which of necessity have no present, as I have previously stated.

The characteristic of the first conjugation is the letter *a* in the second person singular of the present.

INFINITIVE.

Kochać, ' to love.'

INDICATIVE.

Present Tense.

Kocham.	kochasz.	kocha.
Kochamy.	kochacie.	kochają.

Perfect.

For the masculine, add the suffixes for the first and second persons, with the bindevocal *e* to the participial form in *l,* and add them also to the feminine *kochala* and the neuter *kochalo.* For the plural masculine, add the suffixes to *kochali,* and for the feminine and neuter to *kochaly,* thus *kochalem, kochalam, kochalom,* &c.

Pluperfect.

To form this tense, add to the perfect *był* for the mascu-line singular, and *byli* for the plural; *była* for the feminine singular, and *było* for the neuter; and *były* for the plural of both genders.

Future.

Put the auxiliary *będę*—inflecting it regularly, as in the form given under the verb *być*, 'to be,'—before *kochał* for the masculine singular, and *kochali* for plural ; *kochała* for feminine, and *kochało* for neuter singular; and *kochały* for the plural of both, according to the invariable rule.

IMPERATIVE.

Kochaj.
Niech *or* niechaj kocha.
Kochajmy.
Kochajcie.
Niech *or* niechaj kochają.

It will be observed that the characteristic letter of the imperative is *j*, to which the terminations of the plural are added, e. g. *kocha-j-my*.

I have not given at length another form of the impera-tive included in some grammars : it is formed by adding the enclitic *ż* or *ze* to the simple form

CONDITIONAL.

Made by adding the pronoun suffixes to -*by*, which is appended to the participial form, as *kochałbym*. In the plural we have the usual *kochali* and *kochały*, with the personal suffixes.

The pluperfect is formed by adding to the perfect *był*, which is inflected in the manner previously shown.

SUBJUNCTIVE.

Perfect.

This is *aby*, with the usual personal suffixes appended to the inflected participial form in *ł*.

OPTATIVE.

The same, *oby* being added instead of *aby*.

PARTICIPLES.

Pres. kochający.	kochająca.	kochające.
Past, kochany.	kochana.	kochane.
Fut. mający kochać.	mająca kochać.	mające kochać.

GERUND.—*Kochając*, ' loving.'

The tenses, which are wanting to the imperfect verb *kochać*, are supplied by the perfect verb *ukochać*.

SECOND CONJUGATION.

The characteristic of this conjugation is *iesz* or *esz* in the second person singular present.

Grzebać, 'to bury.'

Present.

Grzebię.	grzebięsz.	grzebię.
Grzebięmy.	grzebięcie.	grzebią.

Perfect.

Formed from the participial form *grzebał,* with the addition of the suffixes, as in the preceding verb. The same remarks apply to the pluperfect and future.

IMPERATIVE.

Grzeb.
Niech *or* niechaj grzebię.
Grzebmy.
Grzebcie.
Niech *or* niechaj grzebią.

Also another form with the addition of the enclitic *że.*

CONDITIONAL.—*Grzebałbym.*

Cf. the former under *kochać,* also the pluperfect on the same model.

SUBJUNCTIVE.—*Abym grzebał.* }
OPTATIVE.—*Obym grzebał.* } Cf. with *kochać.*

PARTICIPLES.

Present ... Grzebiący, &c.
Past ... ... Grzebany, &c.
Future ... Mający grzebać. &c.

GERUND.—*Grzebiąc,* 'bringing.'

Other tenses are supplied to this verb by the perfect or complete form *pogrzebać*. Verbs belonging to this conjugation which end in *ować, iwać* and *ywać*, and are generally derivatives, change their termination into *uję, ujesz, uje,* &c., in the present.

The following rules may help to ascertain how the verbs ending in *ać* belonging to this conjugation form their present, this being in reality the only difficulty in the Polish verb :—

When the final consonant of the stem is *b, m, p,* the vowel *i* must be added before the personal suffixes; as,

> Łamię, ' I break,' from *lamać*.
> Łamiész.
> Łamię.
> Łamiemy.
> Łamięscie.
> Łamią.

When the final consonant is *s* or *w*, preceded by another consonant, the *i* is only added to the second and third persons of the singular, and the first and second of the plural; thus—

Zwę, 'I call.'	Zw-i-emy.
Zw-i-esz.	Zw-i-ecie.
Zw-i-e.	Zw-ą.

If the final consonant of the stem is *s*, preceded by a vowel, as *pisać*, 'to write,' this hard consonant is changed into the soft *sz*, as *piszę*, 'I write.' So also other hard consonants which precede *ać* are changed into the soft consonants corresponding to them; as *lgać*, 'to lie,' *łzę*; *plakać*, 'to weep,' *placzę*. When the termination of the stem is *sk*, it becomes *szcz*, as *głaskać*, 'to pat with the hand,' *głaszczę*; so also *r* is changed into *rz*, *t* into *c*, and *z* into *ż*.

In the monosyllabic verbs, *brać*, 'to take,' *prać*, 'to wash linen,' and the verbs compounded from them, *io* is inserted between the first and final consonants of the stem in the first person singular and third person plural; as, *biorę*, *bierzesz*, *bierze*, *bierzemy*, *bierzecie*, *biorą*.

Verbs ending in ąć.

When the root consonant is *d*, in the inflections *m* must be put after it, with the vowel *i* in all the persons, except the first and last, as *dąć*, 'to breathe.'

Dmę.	Dmiemy.
Dmiesz.	Dmiecie.
Dmie.	Dmą.

When the final consonant of the stem is *n*, an *i* must be added to all the persons of the present except the first singular and the third plural, as *pragnąć*, ' to be thirsty ;' the present of which is thus inflected—

Pragnę.	Pragniemy.
Pragniesz.	Pragniecie.
Pragnie.	Pragną.

The present tense of the verbs *ciąć*, ' to cut,' *giąć*, ' to fold,' is thus inflected—

Tnę.	Tniemy.
Tniesz.	Tniecie.
Tnie.	Tną.

The *t* for *c* here being altogether irregular.

In many verbs ending in *nąć*, the *n* disappears entirely in the inflection of the perfect, as *rosnąć*, ' to grow.'

Rosłem.	Rośliśmy.
Rosłes.	Rośliście.
Rosł.	Rośli.

Verbs ending in ec, uc.

Verbs terminated in this way, as *ciec*, ' to flow,' *piec*, ' to cook,' change the consonant *c* into *k* in the present, in the first person singular, and third plural.

Piekę.	Pieczemy.
Pieczesz.	Pieczecie.
Piecze.	Pieką.

Verbs ending in *ić* take *j* after *i* in the present; e. g., from *bić*, 'to fight.'

Biję.	Bijemy.
Bijesz.	Bijicie.
Bije.	Biją.

The same is the case with verbs in *uć* and *yć*, as *czuć*, 'to feel,' *żyć*, 'to live.'

The following verbs belonging to this conjugation are very irregular:—

Jeść, 'to eat.'

Present.

Jem, 'I eat.'	Jemy.
Jesz.	Jecie.
Je.	Jedzą.

Perfect.

Jadłem, 'I ate.'	Jedliśmy, *f.* jadłysmy.
Jadłeś.	Jedliście.
Jadł.	Jedli, *f.* jedly.

Future

(borrowed from perfect form of verb).

Zjem.	Zjemy.
Zjesz.	Zjecie.
Zje.	Zjedzą.

Imperative.

Jedz.	Jedzmy.
Niech je.	Jedzcie.
	Niech jedzą.

Iść, ‘ to go on foot.’

Present.

Idę.	Idziemy.
Idziesz.	Idziecie.
Idzie.	Idą.

Perfect.

Masc.

Szedłem, ‘ I went.’	Szliśmy.
Szedłeś.	Szliście.
Szedł.	Szli.

Fem.	*Plural*
Szłam, szłaś, szła.	(for both genders).
Neut.	Szlyśmy.
Szłom, szłoś, szło.	Szlyscie.
	Szły.

Future.

Przyjdę, ‘ I shall come.’	Przyjdziemy.
Przyjdziesz.	Przyjdziecie.
Przyjdzie.	Przyjdą.

IMPERATIVE.

Idź.   Idźmy.
Niech idzie. Idźcie.
              Niech idą.

It has been thought advisable to give the chief tenses of these verbs on account of their being so much in use.

THIRD CONJUGATION.

The characteristic of this conjugation is that the 2nd pers. sing. present ends in *isz*.

Verbs belonging to this conjugation, which terminate in the infinitive in *ać*, as *bać się*, 'to fear,' change in the present and future *a* into *oj*, in the first person of the singular and the third person of the plural : in the other persons they change *a* into *oi*; e. g. *stać*, 'to stand,' present.

Stoję.   Stoimy.
Stoisz.   Stoicie.
Stoi.   Stoją.

Spać, 'to sleep,' changes *a* into *i* :

Spię.   Spimy.
Spisz.   Spicie.
Spi.   Spią.

They preserve in all the persons of the past tenses *a* before *ł* or *l*; e. g. *bałem się*.

If the stem of a verb ends in *l*, as *myśleć*, 'to think,' the present is thus inflected :

Myślę.   Myślimy.
Myślisz.   Myślicie.
Myśli.   Myślą.

The softening of the final consonants for euphony is shown in the treatment of verbs ending in *ić*, in the first sing. and third plural, as follows:—When a hard consonant ends the stem, the *i* of the infinitive is preserved, as *ziębić*, 'to cool,' *ziębię*, 'I cool,' *ziębią*, 'they cool;' but when a soft consonant goes before, the *i* is not preserved. All these verbs keep in the past tenses their characteristic vowel *i* before *ł* and *l ;* e. g. *prosiłem, prosiliśmy*, &c., 'I entreated.'

Palić, 'to burn.'

INDICATIVE.

Present Tense.

Palę,	palisz,	pali.
Palimy,	palicie,	palą.

Perfect.

Paliłem,	paliłam,	paliłom,

and the other persons as before.

In the plural, add the pronominal suffixes to the plural forms, masc., fem., and neut. of the participle, as previously.

The *Pluperfect*, same as the form in *kochać*.

Future.

Będę palił, &c., as before.

IMPERATIVE.

Pal.
Niech *or* niechaj pali.
Palmy.
Palcie.
Niech *or* niechaj palą.

CONDITIONAL.

Paliłbym, &c.

SUBJUNCTIVE.

Abym palił, &c.

OPTATIVE.

Obym palił, &c.

PARTICIPLES.

Present,	palący,	paląca,	palące.
Past,	palony,	palona,	palone
Future,	mający palić,	mająca palić,	mające palić.

GERUND—Paląc, ' burning.'

Some tenses are supplied to this verb by the perfect form, *spalić.*

FOURTH CONJUGATION.

The characteristic of this conjugation is that the 2nd pers. sing. present ends in *-ysz.*

Słyszeć, 'to hear.'

INDICATIVE.

Present.

| Słyszę | słyszysz | słyszy. |
| Słyszymy | słyszycie | słyszą. |

Perfect—Słyszałem.

Formed in the same way as given in the previous paradigms.

Pluperfect—Same as before.

Future—Będę słyszał, &c.

IMPERATIVE.

Słysz.

Niech *or* niechaj słyszy.

Słyszmy.

Słyszcie.

Niech *or* niechaj słyszą.

CONDITIONAL— Słyszał bym

The pluperfect as in previous paradigms.

SUBJUNCTIVE—Abym słyszał.

OPTATIVE—Obym słyszał.

PARTICIPLES.

Present,	Słyszący,	-a,	-e.
Past,	Słyszany,	-a,	-e.
Future,	Mający słyszeć, &c.		

GERUND—Słysząc, 'hearing.'

Tenses wanting to this verb are supplied by the perfect form, *usłyszeć*; e. g., *usłyszałem*, ' I have heard.'
All verbs in the fourth conjugation end in the infinitive in *eć* or *yć*. Verbs which make the infinitive in *eć* have in the past tenses *a* before *ł*, and *e* before *l*, as *jęczałem*, ' I groaned;' *jęczeliśmy*, ' we groaned.' Those verbs which make the infinitive in *y*, preserve it throughout the perfect tense.

PASSIVE VOICE.

There is no separate form for the Passive Voice in Polish. It may be expressed by the auxiliary *być* and the passive participle; but this method is rare in Polish, which prefers to represent the passive either by a reflexive verb, or by changing the mode of expression and using the active; or employing the third person of the present, or the past participle used impersonally with the accusative of the pronouns *ja, ty, on, my, wy, oni,* or a substantive; thus, instead of saying *oni byli zabijani,* ' they were killed.' it is more in accordance with the Polish idiom to say *zabijano ich :* this is by an idiom of the Polish language, by which, even in the case of a neuter verb, although it has properly no past participle passive, yet one may be employed in an impersonal use, as *skakano,* ' they were leaping' (literally, it having been leapt); *ziewano,* ' they were yawning.' Cf. *Mickiewicz Pan Tadeusz,* Book X. *Że mnie Jackowi czarną podano polewkę,* ' That the black soup was given to me, Jaczek.'

E

The reflexive verb, however, cannot be used for the passive when any ambiguity might arise ; thus we cannot say, *Cezar zabił się dnia pietnastego Marca*, ' Cæsar was killed on the fifteenth of March.' The following enclitics are suffixed to verbs, *li* (which implies a question), and *ż* after vowels, *że* after consonants. The two latter add emphasis to the expression. Similar particles are found in the Russian and Bohemian languages. By an idiom of the Polish language the infinitives *widać*, *słychać*, may be used alone in an impersonal sense, without adding *można*, (it is possible) ; so also in the past tenses we have *było widać*, just as in English, ' there was to be seen.'

Sometimes, instead of *był*, *został* is used with the past participle as an historical perfect, as *stałek zaniesiony został aż ku brzegom Danii* (Baliński), ' the vessel was brought to the coast of Denmark.' Both *jest* and *był* can be omitted by an idiom common to all the Slavonic languages. Every verb has its substantive, as *bity*, ' beaten,' *bicie*, ' the act of beating ;' *proszony*, ' entreated,' *proszenie*, ' the act of entreating :' these substantives are all of the neuter gender, and have no plural. The verbal noun in Polish can take with it the reflexive pronoun ; as *nieudanie się powtórnéy eleckcyi Leczynskiego*, ' the failure of the second election of Leczynski.'

IMPERSONAL VERBS.

Of these there are many in Polish, as *bywa*, ' it happens ;' *grzmi*, ' it thunders.' All verbs may be made impersonal by adding the pronoun *się* to the third person of the present and future of the active verb, and to the third person neuter of the perfect, as *mówi się*, 'it is said,' *mówiło się*, 'it has been said.'

PARTICIPLES.

There are four participles—

Present.

1st. The undeclined, called sometimes the gerund, *czytając*.

2nd. The declined, *czytający*, 'reading.'

Past.

1st. Undeclined or gerund, *dawszy*, 'having given.'

2nd. Declined, *przeczytany*, 'having been read.'

PREPOSITIONS.

Prepositions which govern the genitive :—

Bez, ' without.'

Dla, ' for.'

Do, ' to.'

Około, ' around.'

Krom, okrom, prócz, oprócz, ' outside of.'

Miasto, zamiast, ' in place of.'

Od, ' from.'

Podle, ' near.'

Podług,
Według, } ' according to.'

Śród,
W śród, } ' in the midle of.'

U, ' with ' (cf. the French *chez*).

Also the following adverbs used as prepositions :—

    Blizko, ' near.'

    Niedaleko, ' not far.'

    Obok, ' by the side of.'

    Poprzek, ' across.'

    Wewnątrz, ' within.'

    Zewnątrz, ' without.'

    Wzdłuż, ' along.'

Prepositions which govern the dative :—

    Gwoli,
    Kwoli, } ' for, according to.'

    Ku, ' forward.'

    Przeciw,
    Preciwko, } ' against.'

    W brew, ' against, in contempt of.'

Przez, ' by,' governs the accusative ; *przy,* ' near,' the locative.

Naprzeciw, naprzeciwko, ' against,' ' opposite,' govern the genitive or dative.

Mimo, pomimo, ' in spite of,' ' notwithstanding,' govern the genitive or accusative. *Mimo,* however, when it means ' near,' always governs the genitive.

Z takes the genitive when it marks the place from which the movement comes, the cause, the material out of which a thing is made ; but when it signifies ' together with,' it must take the instrumental.

The prepositions *między, pomiędzy,* 'among;' *nad,* 'upon;' *pod,* 'under;' *przed,* 'before;' *za,* 'beyond,' govern the accusative when motion is signified, but the instrumental when rest is implied. The prepositions *na,* 'on;' *o,* 'about;' *po,* 'after;' *w,* 'in,' govern the accusative when the verb with which they are used marks motion to a place. On the other hand, they govern the locative when the verb with which they are used implies rest.

ADVERBS.

I can only find room here for the principal adverbs : the rest can be learned from the dictionaries.

PRIMARY

Gdzie, ' where.'
Tu, ' here.'
Wnet, ' soon.'
Gdy, ' as.'

DERIVED.

Dobrze, ' well.'
Długo, ' long.'
Słabo, ' weakly.'
Mocno, ' strongly.'

COMPOUNDED.

Nazajutrz, ' the following day.'
W czas, ' at the right time,' ' punctually.'
Przedlem, ' previously.'
Niegdyś, ' once.'

ADVERBS OF TIME.

Zawsze, 'always.'
Nigdy, 'never.'
Teraz, 'now.'
Dawno, 'long since.'

OF PLACE.

Na górze, 'above.'
Na dole, 'below.'
Na podal, 'from afar.'
Na przeciw, 'from opposite.'

OF MANNER.

Po polsku, 'in the Polish manner.'
Zewnątrz, 'from without.'
Ustnie, 'by word of mouth.'
Cichaczém, 'quietly.'

INTERROGATIVE.

Kiedy, 'when?'
Zkąd, 'from whence?'
Gdzie, 'where?'
Dokąd, 'whither?'

AFFIRMATIVE.

Koniecznie, 'certainly;' *ba,* 'yes.'

Adverbs are formed from adjectives by changing the termination of the adjective into *e* or *o;* for example, *wesoły,* 'gay,' *wesoło,* 'gaily.'

Adverbs ending in *ie* are formed from adjectives which have a hard consonant in the last syllable but one, as *pewne*, ' sure,' *pewnie*, ' surely.'

Some adverbs have a double termination, as *śmiało*, or *śmiele*, ' boldly.'

Many adverbs are formed in Polish by the use of sub-stantives, either alone or with prepositions, as *na bakier*, ' across ;' *na jaw*, ' evidently ;' *na oślep*, ' blindly ;' *poprzek*, ' across ;' *pogotowiu*, ' in readiness ;' *wewnątrz*, ' within ;' *wet za wet*, ' tit for tat.' So also substantives alone, as *obłazem*, ' in a body ;' *raptem*, ' suddenly ;' *ukradkiem*, ' secretly ;' *rankiem*, ' in the morning ;' *pospołu*, ' to-gether.'

The comparative of adverbs is formed by adding *j* or *ej* to the stem ; as, *skromnie*, ' more modestly ;' *smieléj*, ' more boldly.' For the superlative add *naj* to the comparative adverb ; as, *piękniej*, ' more beautifully ;' *najpiękniej*, ' most beautifully.'

CONJUNCTIONS.

Of these there are different sorts: some join sen-tences together, as *a, i*, ' and ;' *także, też*, ' also ;' *oraz, tudzież*, ' so that ;' *nie tylko-ale*, ' not only,'—' but ;' *ani—ani*, ' neither.' *A* when employed between two ad-verbs strengthens the expression of the adverb, as *wszyscy a wszyscy*, ' all without exception ;' *nic a nic*, ' absolutely nothing.'

Alternative conjunctions, *albo, lub......albo, lub*, or *bądź......bądź... ..,* ' whether '......, or *czy*, ' if ;' *czyli*, or *czy......czy*, ' whether it be that,' &c. Conjunctions of comparison, *jako......tak*; as, *tak......że*, 'so that;' *niż niżeli* (after the comparative), *raczej .....niż*, 'rather than.'

Adversative conjunctions, such as *acz, aczkolwiek,* 'although,' *ale, lecz,* 'but,' *choć, chociaż,* 'although,' *zaś,* 'but,' which latter, like the Latin *quoque,* is never put as the first word in a sentence. Conditional conjunctions are *byle,* 'provided that,' *chyba,* 'unless.' Conjunctions of time are *gdy,* 'when,' *jak tylko,* 'as soon as.' Optative conjunctions, *bogdaj oby,* 'God grant that,' used to express the optative mood.

CHAPTER III.
Syntax.

As brevity has been aimed at in this Grammar, I shall allow myself to omit those points of Syntax which are not peculiar to Polish, but are shared in by the majority of languages.

CASES OF NOUNS.

1. The genitive is used after many adjectives and participles: of these a few are here specified—the rest must be learned by practice; as, *godzien nagrody,* 'worthy of recompence;' *potrzebujący wsparcia,* 'having need of assistance.'

2. After all the cardinal numbers beginning with *pięć,* 'five.' (See page 17.)

3. The genitive is always used after the verb when it goes with a negative; as *nie czyta listu,* 'he does not read the letter.'

Ale serce u molojców,
Niezlęknie sie Turków.—(*Siemieński.*)

'But the hearts of the young men do not fear the Turks.'

4. After the impersonal verb, *niemasz* or *niema, niebyło*, 'there is not,' 'there was not;' as *nie ma zgody*, 'there is no agreement.'

5. After active verbs where they have a partitive sense; as *daj mi wody*, 'Give me some water.'

6. Verbs compounded of the prepositions *do, od, na, nad, przy, u*, take the genitive; as *nazrywać kwiatów*, 'to gather flowers.'

7. The genitive is used after adverbs implying abundance, or want, as in other languages.

8. Also to express quality or character; as *człowiek wysokiego wzrostu*, 'a man of tall stature.'

9. Also to express point of time; as *Dwadziestego dziewiątego stycznia roku tysiącznego ośmsetnego ośmdziesiątego czwartego*, 'January 29, 1884.'

A great number of verbs take the genitive, but these must be learned by the help of a good dictionary.

The *Dative.*—Many adjectives take the dative, as *posłuszny*, 'obedient.' Verbs compounded with *do* take the dative, and many others which can be learned from the dictionary.

The *Accusative* is, as in most languages, the ordinary case after the verb. The *price* of a thing is put in the accusative, also duration of time, distance, height and length (with these four last compare the Latin use).

The *Instrumental.*—Many verbs take this case ; as *mia-nować go wodzem*, ' to name him leader.'

It is sometimes employed idiomatically with the verb ' to be ;' as *jestem gospodarzem*, ' I am the master.' And the same is the case with *zostawać*, ' to become ;' as *został pielgrzymem*, ' he has become a pilgrim.' The following examples will, it is believed, clearly illustrate the various uses of this case, which is often peculiarly employed in the Slavonic languages :—*jechał nocą*, ' he travelled during the night;' *jadł łyżką*, ' he ate with a spoon ;' *złapał zająca żywcem*, ' he has caught a hare alive ;' *nazywał mnie przyjacielem*, ' he called me friend.'

The *Locative* expresses in what place, or when, except the days of the week, when point of time is marked by the accusative ; as *we czwartek*, ' Thursday.'

ADJECTIVES.

The adjective agrees in number, gender, and case with its substantive. When an adjective refers to the names of a man or a woman, or a man and an animal, it is put in the plural of the more worthy gender ; but when the adjective is placed with several names of inanimate things, of whatever gender they may be, it is used in the neuter plural. In sentences where the two subjects of the verb are connected by the preposition *z*, the verb may be put in the singular or the plural ; as, *ojciec z synem żył w zgodzie*, or *ojciec z synem żyli w zgodzie*, ' the father lived peaceably with his son.'

Collective substantives ending in *stwo* require the verb in the plural. With collective numerals the verb is put in the third person singular, and when in a past tense with the singular neuter; as, *dwoje dzieci umarło,* 'two children are dead.'

PRONOUNS.

Co, 'what,' is often used instead of *ktory,* when it refers not to the subject, but to the whole previous sentence.

Comparison of Adjectives.—If a superior thing is compared with an inferior, the adverbs *niż, niżli, niżeli, aniżeli,* must be used; as *Droższe jest życie aniżeli majątek,* 'Life is more valuable than goods.' But if superiority is attributed to the thing which is the object of the comparison, the adverb *jak* is placed after the comparative; as, *Nie ma nic lepszego jak spokojne sumienie,* 'There is nothing better than a quiet conscience.' Instead of the adverbs *niż, niżli, niżeli, aniżeli,* the preposition *od* may be employed with the genitive, or *nad* with the accusative: *Ja jestem młodszy od ciebie,* 'I am younger than thou.'

VERBS.

The preposition *do* is employed after verbs when it is desired to express an approximate number; as *Było tu do trzy dziestu ludzi,* 'There were here almost thirty men.' *Od* is used to designate the place or the time after which a thing is begun; as, *od piątego roku,* 'from the fifth year.' *Od.* is used after passive participles and neuter verbs, to express the agent or instrument; as *kochany od przyjaciol,* 'loved by one's friends;' *umiera od żalu,* 'he is dying of grief.' *Z* is also used to express the instrument or agent; as *mdleje z słabości,* 'he faints from weakness:' so also *przez*—thus we may equally say *wybrany od wojska,* or *wybrany przez wojsko,* 'elected by the army.'

Nad is used with the instrumental after verbs implying pity, grief, astonishment, or vengeance. The occasions on which the preposition *w* are employed remind us of the difference in Latin between the uses of *in* with the accusative and with the ablative; as *zamienić w chleb,* 'to change into bread;' *oblec w szatę,* 'to surround with a garment.'

The preposition *z* governs the genitive of substantives to express material, as *dom z drzewa,* 'a house of wood,' which can also be expressed by the adjective, as *dom drzewniany;* also to imply motion from, as in English; and it is the ordinary case after the superlative, as *najpilniejszy z nich,* 'the most industrious of them.'

On the Arrangement of Words in a Sentence.

Owing to the Polish language being in a highly synthetic state, great licence is allowed in this respect. Much must depend upon the taste of the writer; and, in order to get a good style in composition, good works should be read, such as Lelewel's "History of Poland," or the "Ballads" of Mickiewicz, which would be useful for the beginner. It may be remarked, however, that a preposition cannot be separated from the noun which it governs, and the adverb must be put either immediately before or after the word which it qualifies. Any conjunction may begin a sentence, except *zaś* and *bowiem*. The verb is frequently put at the end of a sentence. The adjective and participle can be separated, by many words, from the substantives with which they agree. Thus, *Domowe między następcami Karola Wielkego w rozdzielonem cesarstwie rozruchy*, ' The domestic troubles among the successors of Charles the Great in his divided empire.'

In order to convey to the reader a fair idea of the construction of a sentence, the following lines are given, selected from " Lelewel's History of Poland," *Dzieje Polski*, page 58. (Leipzig, 1837) :—

Pomimo opłakanego położenia w jakim się Polska
In spite of the melancholy condition in which herself Poland

znajdowała, nie można powiedzieć aby miała być biedną
found, not is possible to say that she found herself poor

i znędzioną, tylko w niej ładu i publicznego życia niedos-
and miserable, only in her of order and public life was

tawało, które umiał obudzić Łokietek. Ludność Polska
not which understood how to stimulate Lokietek. The people Polish

widocznie wzrastała, liczba wsi i miast pomnożyła się,
visibly increased, the number of villages and cities augmented itself

i wielu Polaków szło w Litwę i na Ruś, fortuny szukać.
and many Poles went to Lithuania and to Russia, fortunes to seek.

Licznych księstw stolice podnożąc się pocięgnęły za
Of many principalities, the capitals raising themselves, drew after

sobą wzrost wielu innych miast. Murowano kościoły
them the growth of many other cities. They built of stone churches

i klasztory a w miastach i domy. Po dworach szla-
and convents, and in the cities also houses. In the abodes belong-

checkich i znamienitszych   wiejskich   domach,   można
ing to gentlemen, and   notable   country   houses   possible

było widzić piece i w ścianie pomieszczone z wyprowad-
it was   to see stoves, and in the wall   placed   with   built

-zoną nad dach szyją kominy, co nie mało, do wygody
up   above roof projection chimneys, which not a little to convenience

i zdrowia przyczyniło.   Okna były niewielkie, ale szklanne.
and health   contributed.   The windows were small, but made of glass.

Szkło rozpowszechniało się.   Obok dawnych drzewnianych,
(The use of) glass spread itself.   By the side of old   wooden,

glinianych lub metalowych kubków i baniek stawały
earthen   or   metallic   goblets and cups   stood

sklenice i butelki.   Polewane gliniane naczynia, coraz w
glasses and bottles.   Glazed   earthen   vessels,   always in

lepszym   gatunku   upowszechniały się.   Do ubioru
the best   style   developed themselves.   For the furniture

i mieszkań, więcej było potrzeba kobierców, wybor-
also of the dwellings more   was   need   of carpets,   most

niejszego sukna i jedwabnych materyj równie po dworach
excellent linen and   silk   materials, equally   at the courts

jak przez mieszczan używanych.
as among the burghers   used.

The following points of syntax in this passage seem·
worthy of special attention:—

Nie można, used impersonally, as explained on page 50.
With this may be compared *było potrzeba*, like the Latin
opus fuit, a few lines further on.

Być biedną :—this construction, very much used in the
Slavonic languages, is explained on page 58.

Życia niedostawało : observe genitive with the negative, page 56.

Wsi, gen. plural of the somewhat irregular fem. noun *wieś,* ' a village.'

Pomnożyła się : observe the dislike of the Polish language to the ordinary passive form.

Wielu Polaków szło, page 59, a curious idiom.

Murowano : this idiom is explained on page 49.

Pomieszczone . . . . . kominy : observe the arrangement of these words, and compare with remarks on page 61.